Look After Yourself

Get Some Exercise!

Angela Royston

www.heinemann.co.uk/library
Visit our website to find out more information about **Heinemann Library** books.

To order:
 Phone 44 (0) 1865 888066
 Send a fax to 44 (0) 1865 314091
 Visit the Heinemann Bookshop at www.heinemann.co.uk/library to browse our catalogue and order online.

First published in Great Britain by Heinemann Library, Halley Court, Jordan Hill, Oxford OX2 8EJ, part of Harcourt Education.
Heinemann is a registered trademark of Harcourt Education Ltd.

Editorial: Sarah Eason and Kathy Peltan
Design: Dave Oakley, Arnos Design
Picture Research: Helen Reilly, Arnos Design
Production: Edward Moore

Originated by Dot Gradations Ltd
Printed and bound in Hong Kong and China by South China

ISBN 0 431 18020 2 (hardback)
07 06 05 04 03
10 9 8 7 6 5 4 3 2 1

ISBN 0 431 18030 X (paperback)
08 07 06 05 04
10 9 8 7 6 5 4 3 2 1

British Library Cataloguing in Publication Data

Royston, Angela
Get some exercise. – (Look after yourself)
1.Exercise – Juvenile literature
I.Title
613.7'1

A full catalogue record for this book is available from the British Library.

Acknowledgements
The publishers would like to thank the following for permission to reproduce photographs: Alamy pp.**21**, **22**, **24**, **24**; Getty Images p.**4**, p.**5** (Arthur Tilley), p.**8** (Jacob Tapeschaner), p.**10** (Lori Adamski Peek), p.**11** (Jade Albert Studios Inc), p.**15** (Simon Wilkinson), p.**16** (Chad Slattery), p.**18** (Zac Macauley), p.**19** (Peter Cade), p.**20** (Steve Lewis), p.**23** (Zac Macauley/Image Bank);

Contents

Words written in bold, **like this**, are explained in the Glossary.

Your body

Running seems an easy thing to do, but it is not as simple as it seems. When you run, you use many **muscles** to move your legs.

Your muscles need **oxygen** to work. You breathe in oxygen when you breathe in air. This book shows how exercise helps your muscles to work better.

Your muscles

Muscles are part of the soft **flesh** that covers your bones. Bend your elbow and clench your fist. Now you can feel the muscles tighten in your arm.
A muscle tightens when it **contracts**.

Most muscles are attached to bones.
One end of the muscle in your
thigh is attached to your
shin bone. When this
muscle contracts, it
bends your knee.

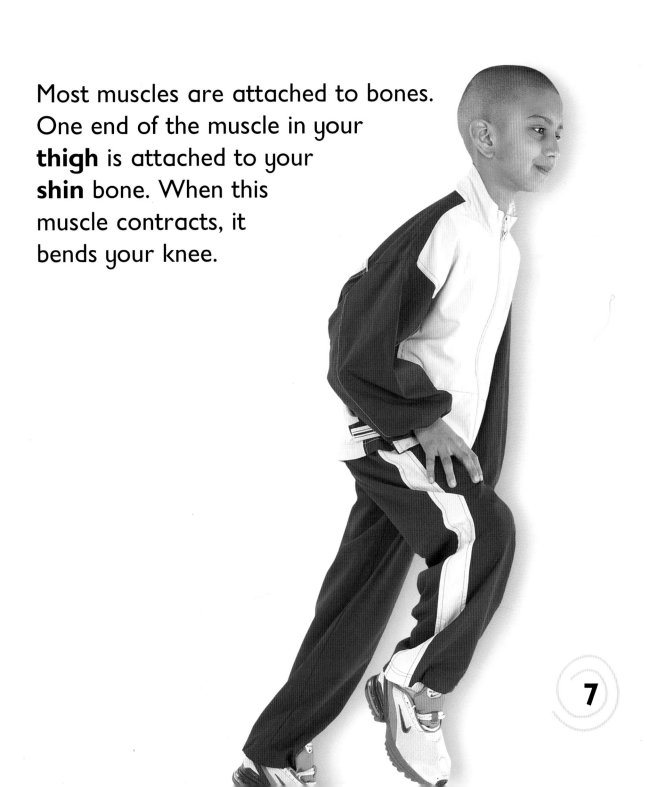

A healthy heart

Muscles use **oxygen** as they work. Your blood takes in oxygen from the air that you breathe in. Your **heart** keeps your muscles supplied with oxygen.

As your heart beats, it pumps blood around your body. The more oxygen your muscles use, the faster your heart beats and the faster you breathe in.

Do exercise that makes you puff

You should do some exercise every day that makes you puff and pant. Run as hard as you can and you will soon start puffing.

Dancing can make you puffed, too. Having to gasp in air makes your **lungs** and **heart** work harder. Your **muscles** also become better at using **oxygen**.

Are you a couch potato?

Don't spend all day playing computer games and watching television. You will become **unfit** and your **heart** and **lungs** will not work so well.

When you do decide to run about, you will quickly get out of breath. Exercise makes your heart work better, so it can supply your **muscles** with more **oxygen**.

Walk, don't drive

Walk to school if you can. Walking is good exercise and it makes you breathe more deeply. This makes your **brain** work better, too.

Always try to walk to where you are going.
It may be more comfortable to travel by car,
but it is not as healthy for you.

Do you take the easy way?

Taking a lift or an **escalator** is an easy way to go up several floors. Climbing stairs is harder work, but it exercises your **muscles**, **heart** and **lungs**.

16

You can get lots of exercise by just doing ordinary things. Do you ever help with the housework? It often involves bending and stretching – good exercise!

Swim as often as you can

Some exercise uses only a few **muscles**. Swimming is very good for your body because it exercises all your muscles at the same time.

The muscles in your arms, legs, stomach and chest move you through the water. Taking in deep breaths exercises your **lungs** and **heart**.

Bend your joints

The parts of your body where your bones move are called **joints**. Playing on the climbing frame strengthens your joints as well as your **muscles**.

When you dance, you use your muscles and your joints. Ballet and **judo** both help you to control your muscles and to keep your **balance**.

Make your body stronger

Exercise makes your body stronger. Stretching your **joints** helps you to move better. Putting your weight on your bones makes them grow stronger.

The more you use your **muscles**, the stronger they become. Strong muscles help you to move faster and further than weak muscles.

Play ball games

Playing with a ball is fun. It also helps you to control your **muscles** and **joints**. You use muscles in your arms, shoulders and back to throw a ball.

Kicking a ball uses many different muscles in your legs and stomach. The more you practise kicking and throwing a ball the more skilled you will become.

Warming up and cooling down

You should stretch your body before you start to exercise. Stretching helps to warm up your **muscles**. It also makes your **joints** move more easily.

When you have finished exercising you should **relax** your muscles to cool them down. Shaking your arms and legs helps to relax the muscles.

It's a fact!

When you are sitting quietly your **heart** beats about 80 times a minute. When you exercise your heart beats faster, about 120 times a minute.

When your heart beats faster, it also pumps more blood with each beat. This means that more blood and **oxygen** reach your **muscles**.

When you are sitting quietly each breath fills less than a quarter of your **lungs**. When you exercise you breathe deeper and faster. This means that you can take in over ten times more air than when you are **relaxed**.

Your body needs oxygen to get energy from the food you eat.

When you exercise your body becomes hotter and you **sweat**. Sweating helps you to cool down. It also means your body loses water. You should drink extra water when you exercise.

Adults' **joints** are stiffer than children's joints. You can probably squat with your feet flat on the floor. Most adults cannot do this. Exercising your joints helps to stop them becoming stiff.

Bread, spaghetti, rice and potatoes are foods that your body needs to make energy. Meat, eggs, cheese and fish are foods that your body needs to build strong muscles.

Glossary

balance   keeping a steady position without falling over

brain   the part of the body that controls the whole body and allows you to be aware of things

contract   tighten and become shorter, to move part of the body

escalator   moving stairway that carries people from one floor to a higher or lower floor

flesh   soft substance that lies between your bones and your skin

heart   the part of the body that pumps blood around

joint   part of the body where two or more bones meet. Joints allow you to bend and move different parts of your body.

judo   sport that practises self-defence

lungs   parts of the body that take in oxygen from the air you breathe in

muscle   part of the body that tightens (contracts) to move a bone or other part of the body

oxygen   gas which all living things need to breathe in to stay alive. Oxygen is one of the gases in the air.

relax   rest your body and mind

shin   bone at the front of your lower leg. It joins your knee to your ankle.

stomach   part of the body into which your food goes when you have swallowed it. Your stomach muscles are over your waist.

sweat   salty water that the body makes in the skin, particularly when you are too hot

thigh   the part of the leg between the knee and the hip

unfit   when your muscles, joints, heart and lungs do not work as well as they should

Find out more

Health Matters: Exercise and Your Health by Jillian Powell (Hodder Wayland, 2002)

Health and Fitness: How Does Exercise Affect Me? by Judy Sadgrove (Wayland, 1999)

Let's Exercise by Elizabeth Vogel (PowerKids Press, 2001)

My Amazing Body: A First Look at Health and Fitness by Pat Thomas and Lesley Harker (Hodder Wayland, 2002)

What About Health: Exercise by Fiona Waters (Hodder Wayland, 2001)

Index